the Soy Milk Cookbook

Delicious & Healthy Non-Dairy Asian Recipes

WU WEN

TUTTLE Publishing

Tokyo | Rutland, Vermont | Singapore

CONTENTS

Hot Pots with Soy Milk Stock

Quick and Easy Noodles with Soy Milk Broth

Soy Milk Rice Porridge: A Chinese Staple

Low-calorie Soy Milk Desserts

Why I Wrote This Book

In recent years soy milk has become popular around the world. Many of us grew up drinking cow's milk, and back in those days you never used to hear soy milk mentioned much. But these days soy milk has become a popular choice for those who are conscious of healthy eating—you can get it easily in cafes and supermarkets, and many recipes for a wide variety of dishes now use soy milk as a key ingredient. In Japan, where I live, yogurt made with soy milk is flying off the supermarket shelves, and products that are made with soy milk boast on their packaging health benefits such as "relieves constipation!" or "lowers cholesterol!"

As someone who grew up in China, I have been familiar with soy milk since childhood, and I could not be happier to see the popularity of soy milk around the world today. That's why I decided to make a cookbook of recipes that use soy milk.

I published my first soy milk cookbook for Japanese readers back in 2010, containing the timeless recipes I love to make. With increasing numbers of soy milk fans around the world, I hope that this new book will bring joy to even more people. As well as my old favorites, this book includes new recipes, and tips on how to incorporate soy milk into what you eat every day. I also share with you some of the healthy habits I've incorporated into my everyday routine.

Soy milk is incredibly good for the body and easy to use in cooking! I truly hope that all of you busy readers will make the most of this wonderful ingredient. And above all, I would be delighted if this book can help you, your families and your loved ones live each day with health and vitality.

—Wu Wen

Soy Milk: Essential for Balancing the Body

I Take Soy Milk for Granted

In the West, most people have grown up drinking cow's milk and using cow's milk in their everyday dishes. The same is true of soy milk in China, where I grew up. We drink cow's milk too. This may be because the concept of eating a good balance of animal and vegetable proteins is deeply rooted in China. But China is also a multi-ethnic country, and there are people who, for religious reasons, avoid animal protein and consciously choose to consume soy milk instead.

In China, the morning starts with soy milk. You can drink it at home, order it at a restaurant, or buy it freshly made at a market stall. For the Chinese, soy milk is a standard breakfast drink throughout the year. It is sometimes served with *youtiao* fried dough sticks, which are sometimes dipped in the soy milk while eating. Naturally, the soy milk used for dipping is also drunk afterward.

Soy milk is a drink I have been consuming every day since as far back as I can remember. To me, soy milk is something so natural that it's simply always been there.

Soy Milk Every Morning

Soy milk and youtiao fried dough sticks are like café au lait and croissants, or miso soup and rice. There are days when I have café au lait, bread and fruit for breakfast, or other days when I might have a Japanese-style breakfast of miso soup, rice and grilled fish. However, soy milk is so natural and familiar to me that I drink it nearly every morning.

Soy milk goes well with bread. I especially like French toast made with baguette and soy milk (see page 18). It's easy to make. Crack the eggs into a bowl or a pot, beat them, and then mix in the soy milk. Cut the baguette into thick slices and add them to the mixture, turning them over occasionally until the baguette has soaked up the egg mixture. If you leave the bread in the egg mixture overnight, it will become even softer and more delicious. In the morning, just take it out of the fridge and fry in olive oil until crispy. It's great served with maple syrup or honey. And don't forget to heat up some soy milk and pour yourself a large mug!

Soy Milk Makes a Delicious Soup Stock

Soy milk can be enjoyed not just as a drink in its own right, but it can also be turned into a delicious soup by simply adding vegetables. For example, warm some soy milk in a pot, toss in some fresh pea shoots, give them a quick simmer, and finish with a sprinkle of salt. Take a sip—you'll be amazed at how the mellow richness of the soy milk combines with the flavor and fragrance of the pea shoots, creating a soup with a gentle sweetness. It's surprising how such a simple step can transform soy milk into an entirely different dish.

By simply changing the vegetables—mushrooms, pumpkin, cauliflower, turnip—you can create a new flavor each time. The umami from the vegetables and the soy milk alone are enough to complete the dish, and from there, just a few dashes of salt or your favorite seasonings will adjust the flavor perfectly.

With soy milk, you can easily make a full-bodied soup without needing any traditional stock. In fact, you could say that soy milk itself is a kind of stock— a pure, natural essence of deliciousness. It's like a dashi stock made from soybeans.

Soy Milk for Beverages, Soups and Mains

If you heat up soy milk you have a delicious drink. If you add something to soy milk, it becomes soup. If you add a few more ingredients, it becomes a main dish. If you can think of soy milk in this way it will feel even easier and more versatile to use.

• **Warm it and drink it right away** I personally love warm soy milk on its own, but you can add a little honey or maple syrup for a touch of sweetness. Beyond the now-popular soy latte, you can enjoy it many other ways—add brown sugar for a brown sugar soy latte, matcha for a matcha soy latte, or cocoa powder for soy milk cocoa. Soy milk drinks aren't just for breakfast; you can enjoy them at any time of day.

• **Add something and it becomes soup** My style is to avoid using much animal protein and to make gentle, soothing soups using seasonal vegetables. Minimal seasoning is enough—and honestly, sometimes no seasoning at all is just perfect.

• **Add a bit more and it becomes a main dish** You can add vegetables, meat, fish or soy products. Soy milk hot pots, pork shabu-shabu, simmered dishes and stews are some of my specialties. If you think of soy milk as a "liquid soup" that doesn't need stock, you'll find the possibilities are endless.

Soy Milk Can Be Sweetened or Unsweetened

Soy milk is the liquid that is squeezed from soybeans, but the soy milk that is generally sold comes in two types, sweetened and unsweetened.

Unsweetened soy milk is made from soybeans and nothing else, and is the liquid that is left over after the *okara* soybean pulp has been removed during the tofu-making process. It has a pronounced soybean flavor with a slight bitterness, allowing you to fully enjoy the natural taste of the soybeans.

On the other hand, sweetened soy milk is made by adding vegetable oils, sugar, salt and other flavorings to unprocessed soy milk to make it easier to drink. It has a subtle sweetness and is recommended for children and people who don't like the distinctive flavor of soybeans.

Both types can be used in cooking and baking, so you can choose based on your preference. If you want to make homemade tofu, for example, you'll need unsweetened soy milk. However, since unsweetened soy milk tends to separate when heated, sweetened soy milk is better suited for recipes that require longer cooking times.

The taste, flavor and concentration of soy milk varies depending on the manufacturer, so it can be fun to try different kinds to find the one you like best.

Sweetened Soy Milk
Unsweetened Soy Milk

Hot Soy Milk Drinks

In China, soy milk drinks are usually served warm. Recently, it has also become popular to add ingredients such as brown sugar and ginger that warm up the body, or to add delicious flavors such as peanut butter or matcha.

Brown Sugar Soy Latte

SERVES 2

1¾ cups (400 ml) soy milk
4 tablespoons dark brown sugar

Put the soy milk in a small pot over medium-low heat. Add the sugar, stirring to dissolve, and bring to a boil. Once it comes to a boil, remove from the heat and serve warm.

Soy Milk Cocoa

SERVES 2

3 tablespoons cocoa powder
2–3 tablespoons raw cane sugar
1¾ cups (400 ml) soy milk

1 Put the cocoa powder and sugar in a small pot. Gradually pour in the soy milk, stirring constantly to dissolve the cocoa and sugar.
2 Place the pot over medium-low heat and bring the mixture to a gentle boil, stirring occasionally. Once it comes to a boil, remove from the heat and serve warm.

Matcha Soy Latte

SERVES 2

1¾ cups (400 ml) soy milk
3 tablespoons matcha powder
2 tablespoons raw cane sugar

Put the soy milk in a small pot over medium-low heat. Add the matcha powder and sugar and stir to dissolve. Once the pot comes to a boil, remove from the heat and serve warm.

Kinako Soy Latte

Kinako roasted soybean flour can be found in Japanese grocery stores.

SERVES 2

1¾ cups (400 ml) soy milk
3 tablespoons kinako roasted soybean flour
2 tablespoons raw cane sugar

Put the soy milk in a small pot over medium-low heat. Add the kinako and sugar, stirring to dissolve, and bring to a boil. Once it comes to a boil, remove from the heat and serve warm.

Brown Sugar Soy Latte
Soy Milk Cocoa
Matcha Soy Latte
Kinako Soy Latte

Soy Milk French Toast

If you use soy milk instead of cow's milk, the aftertaste will be lighter and cleaner. The key to deliciousness is to soak the bread in the soy milk and egg mixture overnight before baking it.

SERVES 2

1 egg
¾ cup (200 ml) soy milk
4 slices baguette, each ¾ inch (2 cm) wide
1 tablespoon olive oil
Maple syrup, to taste

1 Break the egg into a bowl, add the soy milk and beat together.
2 Put the baguette slices in the Step 1 mix. Soak overnight while turning occasionally.
3 Heat the oil in a frying pan and put in the soaked baguettes in a single layer. Pan-fry them until golden brown on both sides.
4 Arrange the baguette slices on plates, and pour maple syrup over them to serve.

Soak the baguettes thoroughly in the soy milk and egg mixture.

Frying in olive oil gives a crisp finish and a distinctive flavor.

Mushroom Soup

When mushrooms are cooked they shrink, so it's best to add more than you think you need. Season simply with just salt and pepper—this really brings out their flavor.

SERVES 2

3½ oz (100 g) enoki mushrooms

3½ oz (100 g) shimeji mushrooms

2 cups (500 ml) soy milk

Salt and coarsely ground black pepper, for seasoning

1 teaspoon toasted sesame oil

1 Cut the root ends off the enoki mushrooms and discard. Cut the enoki in half. Cut the root ends off the shimeji mushrooms and discard. Break the shimeji into small clumps.

2 Put the soy milk and the mushrooms into a pot over medium-low heat. Stir occasionally as the pot comes to a boil. When it comes to a boil, turn the heat to low, partially cover the pot with a lid, and let it simmer for about 10 minutes, taking care not to let it boil over.

3 Season with salt, pepper and toasted sesame oil.

You can find enoki and shimeji (or beech) mushrooms at Asian grocery stores, or at well-stocked supermarkets.

Use plenty of mushrooms. As they simmer, their flavor will dissolve into the soy milk.

Lightly season with salt and pepper, then finish with a splash of toasted sesame oil to add flavor and richness.

Corn Soup

Just mix creamed corn and soy milk and heat it up. This makes a delicious and healthy soup. It's quick and easy to make, so it's perfect when you're busy!

SERVES 2

1¼ cups (300 g) canned creamed corn

1¾ cups (400 ml) soy milk

⅓ teaspoon salt

Black pepper, to taste

½ tablespoon toasted sesame oil

1 Put the creamed corn into a pot, and add the soy milk

2 Stir the mixture over medium-low heat until it comes to a boil. Reduce the heat and simmer for 2–3 minutes. Season with the salt, pepper and toasted sesame oil.

If you want to increase the quantities, use a 4:3 ratio of soy milk to creamed corn.

Finish with a splash of sesame oil to add fragrance—you can also use olive oil instead.

Creamy Yam Soup

This very simple salt-flavored soup is made with soy milk and grated nagaimo yam, also called Japanese or Chinese yam, or mountain yam, which you can find at Asian groceries. A splash of olive oil at the end adds an extra touch of flavor.

SERVES 2

10 oz (300 g) Japanese yam (nagaimo)

1¾ cups (400 ml) soy milk

⅓ teaspoon salt

1 tablespoon olive oil

1 Peel the yam and grate, so that it turns into a paste.

2 Put the soy milk in a pot over medium-low heat. When it comes to a boil, turn down the heat, add the grated yam and stir quickly.

3 Season to taste with the salt. Stir in the olive oil and serve.

You can use a grater or a mortar and pestle to make the yam into a paste.

Add the grated yam to the heated soy milk and mix well.

Add olive oil to finish. I recommend using extra virgin olive oil, which has a nice aroma.

Fluffy Egg and Soy Milk Soup

This is one of our household's go-to soups, made with eggs—often called a complete food—and mineral-rich rock seaweed (or *iwanori*, available at Japanese grocery stores). Iwanori is type of seaweed that grows on rocks, and is more flavorful than regular nori seaweed. You may be able to find iwanori at your Japanese grocery.

SERVES 2

2 eggs
1¾ cups (400 ml) soy milk
¼ teaspoon salt
A little iwanori rock seaweed
½ tablespoon toasted sesame oil

1 Break the eggs into a bowl and mix.
2 Put the soy milk into a pot over medium-low heat, and bring to a boil while stirring. Partially cover the pot with a lid, turn the heat to low, and simmer for 5 minutes, taking care not to let it boil over.
3 Season with the salt, pour in the beaten egg and cook through. Add the iwanori and a splash of toasted sesame oil for fragrance.

Soy Milk Soup with Pea Shoots

This is a quick soup made with pea shoots, a highly nutritious and popular vegetable in China. It's characterized by a gentle thickness added with joshinko rice flour (the non-glutinous type: not sweet mochi rice flour). To preserve their vibrant color and fresh aroma, the pea shoots should be lightly cooked—just enough with residual heat, not overboiled.

SERVES 2

3½ oz (100 g) pea shoots

2 tablespoons non-glutinous rice flour (joshinko)

2 cups (500 ml) soy milk

¼ teaspoon salt

1 teaspoon toasted sesame oil

1 Cut the roots off the pea shoots and discard.

2 Put the rice flour in a pot, add the soy milk and stir to blend.

3 Place the pot over medium-low heat and bring to a boil while stirring. Turn the heat to low and partially cover the pot with a lid. Simmer for 5 minutes taking care not to let it boil over. Season with the salt and toasted sesame oil.

4 Add the pea shoots to the pot and simmer briefly before serving.

Okara Soup

This is an unique dish that uses okara, a by-product of tofu making—it's the pulp that's left over after the soy milk has been extracted from soybeans. You may be able to find okara in a Japanese grocery store, or buy it from a tofu maker.

SERVES 2

½ onion

1 tablespoon untoasted sesame oil

⅓ teaspoon Sichuan pepper powder

2 oz (50 g) okara

2 cups (500 ml) soy milk

⅓ teaspoon salt

1 Slice the onion thinly.

2 Put the sesame oil and Sichuan pepper powder in a pot and heat until fragrant. Add the okara, and sauté well.

3 Pour in the soy milk and bring the pot to a boil. Turn the heat to low, partially cover the pot with a lid, and simmer for 5–6 minutes, taking care not to let it boil over. Season with the salt.

4 Add the sliced onion to the pot and simmer briefly before serving.

Fry the sesame oil and Sichuan pepper until fragrant and then add the okara.

Sauté the okara well, getting rid of any excess moisture.

Add the soy milk and simmer. Season with salt only—since Sichuan pepper is used, there's no need for black pepper.

Curly Endive and Soy Milk Soup

This is a refreshing and distinctive soup made with endive, known for its crisp texture and subtle bitterness.

SERVES 2

1 bunch curly endive, about 7 oz (200 g)

2 slices bacon

½ tablespoon untoasted sesame oil

3 cups (720 ml) soy milk

½ teaspoon salt

Black pepper, to taste

1 Tear the endive into bite-size pieces. Cut the bacon into ⅛ inch (3mm) wide strips.

2 Put the sesame oil and the bacon in a pot and heat. Once the bacon starts to release its fat, add the soy milk and bring to a boil while stirring. Turn the heat to low, partially cover the pot with a lid, and simmer for about 5 minutes, being careful not to let it boil over. Season with the salt and pepper.

3 Add half of the endive from Step 1 to the pot and turn off the heat.

4 Ladle into serving bowls, topped with the remaining endive.

Avocado Soy Milk Soup

A healthy soup made with nutritious avocado. Homemade green onion oil doubles the flavor—it's so good you'll want second helpings!

SERVES 2

1 avocado
1¾ cups (400 ml) soy milk
¼ teaspoon salt

For the green onion oil

½ fat green onion
3½ tablespoons untoasted sesame oil

1 Make the green onion oil. Slice the green onion thinly on the diagonal, place in a frying pan with the untoasted sesame oil and cook slowly until golden brown. Remove from heat just before it burns and transfer to a heatproof bowl.

2 Peel and pit the avocado and cut into bite-size pieces.

3 Pour the soy milk into a pot and place over medium-low heat. When the pot comes to a boil, turn the heat to low, partially cover with a lid, and simmer for about 5 minutes. Add the avocado and simmer for another 2–3 minutes. Season with the salt.

4 Ladle into serving bowls, and top with green onion oil.

Miso Soup with Sweet Potato

The flavor of the soup is enhanced by first sautéing the miso in untoasted sesame oil. The soup is made with Asian sweet potato which has purple skin and white or yellow flesh. You can find them at Japanese and Asian groceries, some farmer's markets and at well-stocked supermarkets.

SERVES 2

7 oz (200 g) Asian sweet potato

1 tablespoon untoasted sesame oil

1½ tablespoons miso

1¾ cups (400 ml) soy milk

1 Wash and thinly slice the sweet potato with the skin on, and put into a bowl of water.

2 Put the sesame oil and miso in a pot and heat. Sauté until fragrant, then add the soy milk and mix well.

3 When the miso has dissolved, drain the sweet potato slices and add to the pot. When the pot comes to a boil turn the heat to low, partially cover the pot with a lid, and simmer for about 10 minutes, being careful not to let it boil over, until the sweet potato is cooked through.

Frying the miso in untoasted sesame oil really brings out its flavor.

Add the soy milk to the miso, gently loosening and dissolving as you stir.

Cut the sweet potato slices thinly so that they cook through easily.

Cauliflower Soup with Shrimp

The cauliflower is cooked with crisp, savory dried shrimp (available in Asian groceries). The oil, which has absorbed the aroma of the dried shrimp, is the secret to this dish's flavor.

SERVES 2

⅓ cauliflower, about 6 oz (170 g)

2 cups (500 ml) soy milk

¾ oz (20 g) dried shrimp

1 tablespoon untoasted sesame oil

Salt, for seasoning

½ tablespoon cornstarch or potato starch dissolved in 2 tablespoons water

1 Cut the cauliflower into 4 wedges.

2 Put the cauliflower in a pot with the soy milk over medium-low heat. When the pot comes to a boil, turn the temperature to low and partially cover the pot with a lid. Simmer for about 10 minutes taking care not to let it boil over.

3 Make the crispy dried shrimp. Chop the dried shrimp roughly, place in a frying pan with the untoasted sesame oil, and sauté until crispy.

4 When the cauliflower is cooked through, season with salt and thicken the soup with the cornstarch slurry.

5 Ladle the soup into serving bowls, and top with the Step 3 crispy fried shrimp, oil and all.

To prevent the contents from boiling over, partially cover the pot with a lid.

Fry the dried shrimp until they are crispy. The frying oil will also become fragrant from the shrimp.

The cornstarch-and-water mix is used to thicken the soup.

Creamy Kabocha Soup

Simmer kabocha pumpkin in soy milk, then use a blender to create a smooth, creamy potage. My way of adding flavor is to use Chinese five-spice powder.

SERVES 2

7 oz (200 g) kabocha squash (weighed after peeling and deseeding)

2 cups (500 ml) soy milk

1 teaspoon chicken stock

⅓ teaspoon five-spice powder

Salt, for seasoning

1 Remove the seeds and pulp from the pumpkin, peel off the skin, and cut the flesh into bite-size pieces.

2 Put the squash pieces, soy milk and chicken stock in a pot over medium-low heat. When it comes to a boil, turn the heat to low, partially cover the pot with a lid and simmer for 7–8 minutes, taking care not to let it boil over. Season with the five-spice powder and salt.

3 Let the pot cool down. Transfer the contents of the pot to a blender, and blend until smooth. You can heat it up again before serving if needed.

Cut the kabocha squash into bite-size pieces, removing the seeds, the pith and the skin. Since the pieces will be blended later, it doesn't really matter how you cut them.

Simmer the pumpkin in soy milk, and season with five-spice powder and salt. Even a small amount of five-spice powder will give off a strong aroma, so about ⅓ teaspoon is enough.

Transfer to a blender and blend until smooth. Once it reaches a creamy consistency, it's ready. You can return it to the pot and reheat before serving if desired.

Soy Milk Soup with Potato

Potatoes gently simmered in soy milk turn out fluffy and tender! Seasoning them simply with salt brings out their natural flavor. A touch of fragrant black pepper is also key to enhancing the taste.

SERVES 2

2–3 medium potatoes

¾ cup (200 ml) water

1¾ cups (400 ml) soy milk

½ teaspoon salt

20 whole black peppercorns, coarsely crushed

1 Peel the potatoes, and soak in water to cover for 5–10 minutes.

2 Drain the potatoes and put into a pot with the ¾ cup of water over heat. When the pot comes to a boil, lower the heat, partially cover the pot with a lid, and simmer for about 10 minutes, taking care not to let it boil over.

3 Add the soy milk to the pot and bring back to a boil while stirring. Turn the heat back down to low, partially cover the pot with a lid, and simmer for another 15 minutes. Season with the salt.

4 Pour in to bowls and serve garnished with the crushed black pepper.

Start by cooking the potatoes in water.

When the potatoes are 60–70% cooked, add the soy milk, and gently simmer to bring out their full flavor.

My Tips for a Healthy Lifestyle

Starting the Day Well

When I wake up in the morning, I go to the kitchen first to boil some water and drink it. In winter, I make it extra hot and drink it from a heat-resistant glass, blowing on it to cool it down. In summer, when it's too hot to drink boiling water, I drink it a little cooler. But I never drink anything colder than my body temperature, so no cold water. I drink a large glass of it, about 2 cups (500 ml), slowly.

After that, I take a shower and get ready for breakfast. While I'm doing this, the water circulates through my whole body, and I feel refreshed and clean inside. I think it's good to give your internal organs a morning shower too—that's the sensation. After digesting the previous evening's dinner, drinking fluids before putting more food into your body helps clean out your system and stimulates your organs, which I feel improves circulation.

Mornings are always busy for most of us. But it's important to start the day as you mean to go on. If you can make an effort to incorporate healthy habits into the start of your day, they will become a part of your routine, and before long they won't feel like an effort at all.

Soy Milk Soup Is a Healthy Breakfast

So, after the hot water, what should you put into your body? I always eat fruit, and then protein. I often go for plant-based protein in the form of soy milk or soy milk soup, and if I want to add animal protein, it's usually just yogurt.

In China and Japan, soup is a common breakfast dish, and one thing I really like to eat in the morning is a simple vegetable soup. A warm soup gently slips into your stomach without burdening your body, then spreads through you, switches your body "on," and helps you start the day smoothly. In winter especially, it's a great way of warming the body and getting it moving properly. Sometimes I whip it up quickly in the morning, or I make it ahead of time while preparing dinner, just tossing leftover vegetables into a pot. The basic ingredients I use are just vegetables, water and salt. Fundamentally, what humans need are fluids, fats, and salt. By adding vegetables to water, you get vitamins and minerals, and by seasoning with salt, you can get the necessary salt intake. Soups are really clever, aren't they?

There's no need to worry about planning your breakfast meals. Just drink plenty of warm fluids in the morning.

Soy Milk Rice Porridge

In China, our breakfast is basically soy milk and rice porridge. The porridge isn't just made with white rice—it changes every day. It could be brown rice, black rice, red rice, millet, foxtail millet or rolled barley. The reason we eat a variety of grains in the morning is because they're nutritious. Making porridge in the morning may sound like a hassle, but it isn't really. It's just like cooking rice and takes about the same time, roughly 20 minutes.

In China, our concept of porridge is a little different from what you might be used to. Our porridge is quite liquid, and we say that we "drink" porridge rather than "eat" it. Chinese-style porridge is made with three times the amount of water for every handful of rice, so it really is more like a soup.

Many of our porridges are made with soy milk. If you're used to oatmeal porridge, try my recipe for Oatmeal Soy Milk Porridge on page 101. I find that oatmeal goes much better with soy milk than with cow's milk, as oatmeal and soy milk are both plant-based. Salt is all you need to season it.

The Benefits of Soy Milk

It is said that tofu was first made in China around two thousand years ago, and that soy milk had already existed before that. It is thought that tofu was introduced to Japan from China during the Nara period (710–794), and that *tofu-yo*, which is said to be the original form of soy milk, first appeared on Japanese dining tables during the Kamakura period (1185–1333).

What is the appeal of soy milk, which has been drunk since ancient times? I think it's not only the unique flavor and aroma, but also how well it helps regulate the body. In the past, there was no nutritional analysis, of course, so people probably continued drinking it just because their bodies felt good from it.

Modern nutritional science also attests to the benefits of soy milk. Soy milk is low in calories and high in protein, so it is effective in preventing lifestyle diseases. Soy isoflavones may help prevent cancer and osteoporosis; lecithin and saponin are said to help prevent brain aging and promote healthy skin; and oligosaccharides help regulate gut health, so they may relieve constipation. Soy milk is also rich in skin-friendly vitamins like B1, B2, B6 and vitamin E. Soy milk is full of health benefits, so it's worth making it a regular part of your diet.

Key Points for Cooking with Soy Milk

Soy milk is easily scorched, so heat it slowly over low heat, stirring it as it comes to a boil. If you suddenly turn up the heat, the proteins can coagulate quickly and cause the soy milk to scorch. If you heat it slowly, it will taste better. Even after it comes to a boil, be careful with the heat.

If you're using thick soy milk and it quickly forms a skin or is too dense to handle like a liquid, try thinning it with water before using. This method is also recommended if you don't want the soy milk to have a strong aroma. It can make soy milk dishes more palatable for people who aren't fond of its taste. If you leave it on the heat for too long, the moisture will evaporate, so take this into account and adjust accordingly.

Another key point is to avoid adding too much seasoning. If you want to bring out the natural sweetness of soy milk, salt is the best option—I can't emphasize this enough. Good salt will bring out the natural flavor of soy milk and enhance its umami. If you're eating something just because it's good for you, you'll get bored. But soy milk dishes are always delicious when they're made well.

The Ingredients Are the Stars of the Dish

My cooking is very simple. I don't use many ingredients in one dish, and I only use essential seasonings, nothing too unusual. The point is that the ingredients are the stars. If you don't make the seasonings the main focus, you're less likely to get tired of the dish, and you can really taste and appreciate the natural flavor and strength of the ingredients.

I recommend that you always try to use ingredients in season, when they're at their peak in both flavor and nutrition. They only need a little seasoning to bring out their best.

Soy milk needs minimal seasoning too, so that its flavor can shine. Soy milk dishes are the ultimate in simple cooking.

If you do want to enhance the natural flavor of the soy milk, try adding a little dried shrimp (see, for example, Cauliflower Soup with Shrimp, page 34); or chicken stock (see Creamy Kabocha Soup, page 36). Dishes like these are a great way to convert any soy milk doubters!

A Balanced Diet of Three Meals a Day

Chinese people—including me—don't really have a habit of eating snacks, so we make sure to eat three proper meals a day. Even in kindergartens and daycare centers, snacks are usually just a small piece of sweet potato. That's because if you eat between meals, you won't be hungry at dinner time.

The general rule for eating is: eat a lot in the morning, eat something good at lunch, and eat lightly in the evening. Since you're going to be active during the day, having a hearty breakfast helps wake up your brain and body by supplying glucose, the brain's main source of energy.

As for "something good" at lunch, this means a nutritionally good meal that contains protein and vitamins. Soy milk soup and vegetables are great options. If you eat too much, you'll get sleepy, so try to keep portions moderate. Then eat even less at dinner time. Since you're just going to sleep after dinner, your body doesn't require much energy. I also cut back on carbs like rice and bread at dinner time. Let your internal organs rest while you sleep.

The Importance of Oil in Your Diet

Oil is essential for the creation of body cells and for helping our bodies absorb vitamins. However, not just any oil will do. The best oils for the body, and those which taste best, are made from a single ingredient using a reliable production method. These include sesame oil, olive oil and rice oil.

The two oils I always have on hand are sesame oil and olive oil. There are two main types of sesame oil, and I use both in the recipes in this book. Toasted sesame oil is a dark-colored oil with a strong aroma, and is often used for finishing recipes. Untoasted (also labeled as "light" or "pure") sesame oil is a clear-colored oil with almost no aroma or particular taste, and is good for frying. For olive oil, I use a fragrant, first-press extra virgin variety.

Taking in healthy oils makes both the body and skin feel more hydrated. Especially as you get older, if you don't moisturize from the inside, you start to feel like a dried fish! I love good butter too, especially on bread, but for cooking, I mainly use plant-based oils.

Five Colors and Five Flavors

"Five colors and five flavors" is a concept from China's Five Elements theory. The five colors are white, black, green, red, and yellow, and the five flavors are sweet, spicy, salty, bitter, and sour. Simply put, the idea is that if you regularly eat a combination of these five colors and five flavors, your health will naturally be maintained. This philosophy is seen reflected in the food of other Asian countries. In Japan, for example, there is a dish called *gomoku gohan* (five-ingredient rice), based on rice, combined with ingredients like shiitake mushrooms, carrots, and snow peas, each with different colors and flavors, to balance nutrition and taste. Korean bibimbap works the same way.

That said, incorporating all of the five colors and five flavors into a single meal is tough, so think in terms of a whole day, or even across a week. Or just try to be mindful at breakfast and dinner—and eat whatever you like for lunch. Don't put too much stress on yourself to follow the rule, otherwise it won't be sustainable.

Soy milk corresponds to the "yellow" category. Yellow foods are believed to boost immunity. Using soy milk as a base and adding green leafy vegetables or white root vegetables is a great way to achieve nutritional balance effortlessly.

In China, the idea of "food as medicine" is deeply rooted, and people believe that eating the right food every day can help to improve their health and prevent illness. The easiest way to put this idea into practice is to eat seasonal ingredients. It's based on the belief that seasonal foods align with what our bodies naturally need at that time of year.

For example, cucumbers and eggplants, which are in season in summer, are high in water content and help cool the body while replenishing fluids. Watermelon is also excellent for hydration and natural sugars. Root vegetables and green onions, which are in season in winter, help warm the body and are perfect for cold weather. Ginger and *chenpi* dried tangerine peel (see page 99) are used to help prevent colds. By eating the seasonal foods that nature provides, you can naturally regulate your body's condition.

Soy milk soup also adapts well to the seasons: in spring, it pairs nicely with watercress or celery; in summer, tomatoes work well. In fall, you can add mushrooms or sweet potatoes; in winter, cauliflower, daikon, or turnip are great choices. Just by using soy milk as a base and adding seasonal vegetables, you're already practicing "five colors and flavors." Eating seasonal produce in its natural form is the best way to stay healthy.

Keeping the Body Warm

Coldness is the source of all kinds of illness. That's why I try not to eat anything that is colder than my body temperature. If my internal organs get cold, my body temperature will drop and my immunity will weaken, making me susceptible to various illnesses.

So, is it enough to just eat warming foods such as green onions or ginger? Not exactly—what matters most is temperature. While some ingredients are believed to warm the body through their natural properties, more importantly, I recommend eating food that's warmer than your body temperature to protect yourself from getting chilled. It's not about warming up after your body is already cold—it's about building a body that doesn't get cold in the first place.

The most basic thing I do is to eat heated food. However, not all cold food is bad. As long as you don't eat it raw, that's fine. For tofu, eat it hot or stewed rather than cold, and when you eat watermelon or tropical fruit, accompany it with a drink of hot tea. This will bring balance.

Also, while fish is often thought to be healthier than meat, fish don't live on land—so for us land-dwelling humans, they're kind of like aliens. That's why I think we need to be mindful of how we eat fish. Foods that live in water are better grilled, simmered, or steamed rather than eaten raw like sashimi. Cooking them protects the body from getting chilled.

As we age, I think it's best to just go with the flow of nature, accept it, and enjoy what we can do. It's not like we're going to become Olympic athletes at this point, and if we can't do something, there's no need to force ourselves to keep at it. The most important thing is to eat in a way that makes us feel good. And only you can know what feels good to *you*. I want to build a mind and body that can recognize that feeling.

Pork, Clams and Daikon Simmered in Soy Milk

In China, pork and clams are often paired together, and the flavor that results from the combination of meat and seafood is truly exceptional. The soy milk soup, infused with their rich umami, is delicious—and the daikon, soaked in all that flavor, is absolutely outstanding!

SERVES 2

7 oz (200 g) block pork belly
7 oz (200 g) Manila clams, weighed with shells on
1 piece daikon radish, about 14 oz (400 g)
1 teaspoon untoasted sesame oil
½ teaspoon whole Sichuan peppercorns
2 tablespoons sake
1¾ cups (400 ml) soy milk
½ teaspoon salt
Finely chopped green onion, for garnish
4–5 green onions, minced

1 Cut the pork belly into ½ inch (1 cm) pieces. Rinse any sand from the clams, and clean them by rubbing their shells together. Drain.
2 Peel the daikon radish, cut in half lengthways, then cut into half-moon slices, ½ inch (1 cm) thick.
3 Put the sesame oil and the Sichuan peppercorns in a pot over heat. When the oil is fragrant add the pork, and pan-fry on both sides until the pork has changed color. Add the clams, sprinkle in the sake, add the daikon radish and stir-fry.
4 Pour in the soy milk, bring the pot to a boil, then turn the heat to low. Partially cover the pot with a lid and simmer for about 15 minutes, being careful not to let it boil over. Season with the salt.
5 Place into individual serving bowls and sprinkle with the green onion.

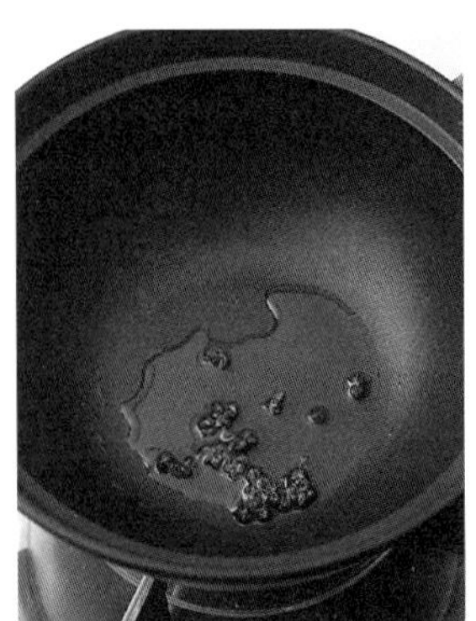

Heat the Sichuan peppercorns in the oil, to infuse the oil with flavor.

Add the pork and sear both sides to lock in the umami. Searing the meat first also keeps it from drying out during simmering.

Soy Milk Mapo Tofu

This is a meatless version of mapo tofu, a Chinese dish that's very popular in Japan. Tofu is simmered in a spicy sauce flavored with Chinese ingredients—douchi fermented soybeans, doubanjiang spicy soybean paste, and Sichuan pepper powder—which you can find in your Chinese grocery store or at well-stocked supermarkets. The dish is topped with fresh green shiso leaves, sold at Asian groceries or farmers markets.

SERVES 2

1 block silken tofu, about 12 oz (350 g)

2 teaspoons douchi fermented soybeans

½ tablespoon untoasted sesame oil

4 inch (10 cm) length green onion, minced

1 teaspoon doubanjiang spicy soybean paste

⅔ cup (150 ml) soy milk

½ tablespoon kudzu powder* or cornstarch, dissolved in ½ tablespoon water

½ teaspoon toasted sesame oil

⅓ teaspoon Sichuan pepper powder

Shredded green shiso leaves, for garnish

1 Cut the tofu into bite-size pieces and drain in a colander. Roughly chop the douchi.

2 Put the untoasted sesame oil and green onion in a wok or frying pan over medium heat. When fragrant, add the douchi and doubanjiang and sauté together to bring out their aroma.

3 Add the tofu to the pan, then pour in the soy milk. When it comes to a boil, turn the heat to low, and partially cover the pan with a lid. Simmer for about 10 minutes, not letting it boil over.

4 Add the kudzu and water mixture to the pan to thicken the sauce. Season with the toasted sesame oil and the Sichuan pepper.

5 Serve topped with shredded green shiso leaves. If you can't get hold of shiso leaves, try Thai basil or mint instead.

***NOTE**

Kudzu powder is a starchy substance from the root of the kudzu plant, used as a thickener in Japanese cooking. You may be able to find it in natural food stores or Japanese groceries, labeled "kudzu starch" or "kudzu powder."

The key to flavor is thoroughly sautéing the green onion, douchi and doubanjiang to bring out their full aroma.

Mapo tofu is usually made with meat, but this delicious vegetarian version uses just tofu as the main protein.

Soy milk gives a smooth, gentle finish to this dish.

Meatballs in Sake Lees and Soy Milk

This large, tender meatball is gently flavored with a soup containing sake lees, also called *sake kasu*, the solid residue left over after sake is pressed. You can buy sake lees in Japanese grocery stores, or sometimes they can be sourced directly from sake breweries.

SERVES 2

2 cups (500 ml) soy milk
2 tablespoons sake lees
⅓ teaspoon salt

For the meatballs

7 oz (200 g) ground pork
Black pepper, to taste
1 tablespoon sake
½ beaten egg
1 oz (30 g) fresh breadcrumbs
⅓ teaspoon five-spice powder
¼ teaspoon salt
1 teaspoon cornstarch or potato starch
½ tablespoon toasted sesame oil

1 Make the meatballs. Put the ground pork in a bowl, and add the pepper, sake, beaten egg, fresh breadcrumbs, five-spice powder, salt, starch and toasted sesame oil in that order, mixing with each addition. Divide the mixture into 2 equal portions and shape each portion into a ball.

2 Put the soy milk in a pot over medium-low heat. When it comes to a boil, add the meatballs and lower the heat, partially cover the pot with a lid, and cook for about 5 minutes, making sure that it doesn't boil over.

3 Add the sake lees and stir gently to dissolve. Then simmer for another 5 minutes. Season with the salt, and serve.

Adding five-spice powder to the meatball mixture gives this dish a distinctively Chinese flavor.

Divide the mixture in half and shape each portion into a large meatball using both hands.

Add the sake lees and stir gently to dissolve. You can also dissolve the sake lees in a little soy milk before adding to the pan.

Yuba and Fried Tofu in Fermented Soy Milk

Yuba is tofu "skin" that forms during the tofu-making process, and is peeled off and dried—it can be bought readymade in Asian groceries. This recipe uses Chinese yuba (as opposed to the Japanese type), which has a satisfyingly chewy texture. You can find most of the ingredients for this dish at your Asian grocery store.

SERVES 2

- 2 oz (60 g) dried Chinese yuba
- 1 block atsu-age thick fried tofu, about 10 oz (300 g)
- ½ burdock root, about 3 oz (80 g)
- 1 oz (30 g) fermented tofu
- 1 tablespoon brine from the fermented soy milk
- ½ tablespoon untoasted sesame oil
- ½ tablespoon toasted sesame oil
- 1¾ cups (400 ml) soy milk
- 1 tablespoon ground white sesame seeds

1 Soak the yuba in water to cover overnight, then cut into ½ inch (1 cm) lengths. Cut the atsu-age tofu into bite-size pieces. Peel the burdock, cut into matchsticks, soak in water for about 5 minutes, then drain.

2 Mix the fermented tofu with 1 tablespoon of its brine to make a smooth paste.

3 Put the untoasted sesame oil and toasted sesame oil in a pot over heat, and when fragrant, add the burdock and stir-fry.

4 Once the burdock has become fragrant, add the yuba and atsu-age tofu, stir-fry briefly, then pour in the soy milk. When the pot comes to a boil, reduce the heat to low, put a lid on the pot and cook for about 5 minutes, taking care that it doesn't boil over. Add the Step 2 paste to season. Sprinkle with white sesame seeds to serve.

Chinese yuba is soaked in water before use. This is called *fuzhu,* a dried, stick-shaped yuba that has been twisted and dried.

To prepare the fermented tofu, mix it with some of its brine to loosen it into a paste. You can adjust the amount to your liking.

Sauté the burdock root well in oil to bring out its aroma while also drawing out its umami.

White Fish and Napa Cabbage in Spicy Soy Milk

This dish, which goes well with rice, has a punchy flavor from the umami of the dried shrimp and doubanjiang spicy soybean paste (see page 56). Dried shrimp is sold in Asian supermarket. You can also use fresh shrimp, squid or scallops in addition to red snapper.

SERVES 2

2 pieces red snapper, about 6 oz (160 g) total

¼ large napa cabbage

1 oz (30 g) dried shrimp

1 tablespoon untoasted sesame oil

1 tablespoon sake

1 teaspoon doubanjiang (see page 56)

2 cups (500 ml) soy milk

Salt, for seasoning

1 teaspoon cornstarch or potato starch dissolved in 1 tablespoon water

1 Cut the red snapper into bite-size pieces. Cut the napa cabbage in half lengthwise.

2 Heat the dried shrimp and untoasted sesame oil in a pot. When fragrant, add the sake and the doubanjiang and stir-fry.

3 When the doubanjiang becomes fragrant, add the 2 halves of napa cabbage, and pour in the soy milk. When the pot comes to a boil, lower the heat, partially cover the pot with a lid, and simmer for about 20 minutes, taking care not to let it boil over.

4 Add the red snapper and simmer for a further 7–8 minutes to cook through. Season with salt and thicken with the starch dissolved in water.

Stir-frying the doubanjiang gives it a deeper flavor and makes it tastier.

Cut the napa cabbage lengthways and add it to the pot as it is. If it doesn't fit, cut it down to the size of the pot.

Thicken the soup slightly with the cornstarch slurry so the soy milk clings nicely to the cabbage when eaten.

Chicken Soy Milk Stew

This healthy version of a popular Japanese-style stew is made with soy milk instead of the usual cow's milk. Using olive oil in the roux gives it a clean, elegant flavor. It's so delicious you're sure to want a second helping!

SERVES 2

1 boneless chicken thigh, about 9 oz (300 g)
1 onion
½ head broccoli
2 cups (500 ml) soy milk
2 tablespoon sake
2 tablespoons olive oil
1 tablespoon flour
⅔ teaspoon salt
A little black pepper

1 Cut the chicken into bite-size pieces. Slice the onion crosswise into 4 slices. Divide the broccoli into small florets, blanch briefly and drain.
2 Put the soy milk, sake, chicken and onion in a pot over medium-low heat. When it comes to a boil, turn the heat to low, partially cover the pot with a lid, and simmer for about 5 minutes, taking care that it doesn't boil over.
3 To make the roux, put the olive and flour into a frying pan over medium heat. Mix well to blend, then remove from the heat.
4 Add the roux to the Step 2 pot. Simmer until slightly thickened, and season with the salt and pepper. Add the blanched broccoli and simmer briefly before serving.

Simmer the chicken and onions in soy milk and sake over low heat, making sure not to let it boil over.

Fry olive oil and flour together to make the roux. It's lighter than using butter.

Add the roux to the pot and cook until it becomes loose and thick. This will make the texture creamy.

Simple Soy Milk Savory Custard

To fully enjoy the flavor and smooth texture of soy milk, this dish is intentionally steamed plain, without any added ingredients, apart from a simple topping of shirasu sardines tossed in sesame oil and parsley.

SERVES 2

2 eggs
½ teaspoon salt
1¾ cups (400 ml) soy milk

For the dressing

2 tablespoons shirasu baby sardines (see below)
1 tablespoon minced parsley
1 tablespoon toasted sesame oil

1 Make the dressing by mixing all the dressing ingredients together in a bowl.
2 In a separate bowl, beat the eggs, season with the salt, and add the soy milk to make a smooth mixture. Strain the mixture through a fine-mesh colander into 2 heat-resistant serving bowls.
3 Put in the bowls into a preheated steamer for 5 minutes. Reduce the heat to low and steam for a further 10 minutes.
4 Remove the bowls from the steamer. Garnish with the dressing and serve.

Shirasu baby sardines can be found at Japanese or Asian groceries, labeled "shirasu," "kama-age shirasu," or sometimes "whitebait."

The key feature of this custard is the minimal use of added flavoring ingredients.

For the best results, start by steaming the custard over high heat for 5 minutes, then low heat for 10 minutes.

Hot Tofu with Soy Milk

This is the simplest recipe for a hot pot dish, where tofu is simmered gently in soy milk. I've given two Chinese-style sauces as accompaniments; it also goes well with readymade ponzu bottled sauce.

SERVES 2

1 block silken tofu, about 12 oz (350 g)

2 cups (500 ml) soy milk

For Sauce A

½ tablespoon doubanjiang spicy soybean paste (see page 56)

1 tablespoon toasted sesame oil

For Sauce B

2 tablespoons white sesame paste

⅓ teaspoon salt

1 Make Sauces A and B by combining the respective ingredients.

2 Put the silken tofu in a pot and cut into 4–6 equal pieces with a knife.

3 Add the soy milk to the Step 2 pot, and simmer over low heat until the soy milk is just about to boil. Remove from the heat.

4 Serve in bowls with Sauce A or Sauce B on top, whichever you like.

Mix doubanjiang and toasted sesame oil to make a sauce. Just salt + toasted sesame oil is also delicious as a sauce.

Silken tofu breaks apart easily, so cut it up after putting it in the pot.

Fu and Turnip Hot Pot with Soy Milk

The main ingredient in this comforting hot pot is wheat gluten, called *fu* in Japanese. With its high protein content, fu was originally used in Zen Buddhist vegan cuisine as a meat substitute. You can find the gluten wheels used in this recipe in your Japanese grocery, as well as the readymade ganmodoki tofu fritters. The small, round Asian turnips used here are sometimes called Hakurei turnips or Tokyo turnips.

SERVES 2

2 small, round Asian turnips
Turnip greens, for garnish
2 cups (500 ml) soy milk
4–6 readymade ganmodoki tofu fritters
½ teaspoon salt
5–6 slices kuruma-fu Japanese dried wheat gluten wheels, about 2 oz (60 g) total

1 Peel the turnips and slice thinly. Finely chop the turnip greens.
2 Put the soy milk, ganmodoki and turnips in a pot over medium-low heat. Bring to a boil, turn the heat to low and season with the salt. Add the fu and partially cover the pot with a lid. Simmer for about 20 minutes, being careful not to let it boil over.
3 Serve in individual bowls topped with the turnip greens.

Slice the turnips thinly. You can use daikon radish instead of turnips.

Add the fu while it is still dry. As it cooks, it will absorb the soy milk and become soft.

Gyoza Dumpling Hot Pot

A hearty hot pot dish made with classic gyoza dumplings, which in China are served both as a side dish and as part of a main meal. Topped with a generous portion of julienned carrot, this one-pot meal provides balanced nutrition on its own.

SERVES 2

1 packet gyoza dumpling skins

1 carrot

2 cups (500 ml) soy milk

½ teaspoon salt

For the gyoza filling

7 oz (200 g) ground pork

Black pepper, to taste

1 tablespoon sake

1 small piece ginger, finely minced

1 tablespoon soy sauce

½ tablespoon toasted sesame oil

1 Make the gyoza filling. Put the ground pork in a bowl, and add the black pepper, sake, ginger, soy sauce and toasted sesame oil in that order, mixing well between additions.

2 Moisten the edges of each gyoza skin with water, put in the appropriate amount of Step 1 filling, and wrap it up while gathering the folds.

3 Julienne the carrot.

4 Put the soy milk in a pot over medium-low heat. When the pot comes to a boil, turn the heat to low, add the Step 2 filled gyoza dumplings and put a lid on the pot. Cook for about 5 minutes taking care that the pot doesn't boil over. Season with the salt.

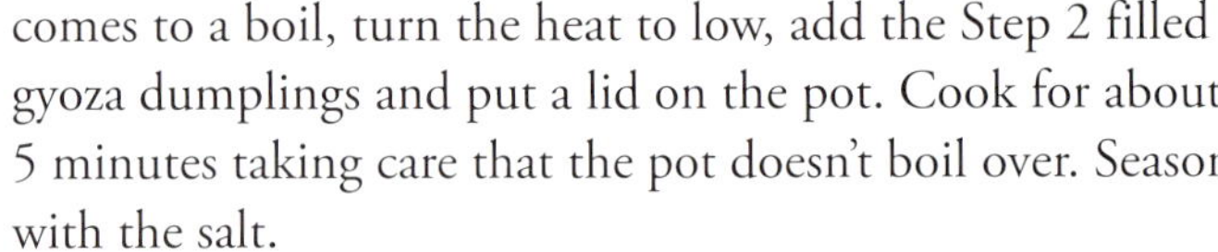

5 Serve in individual bowls with the shredded carrot on top.

Make sure you put just the right amount of filling on each gyoza skin.

Fold the edges inwards and seal the dumplings tightly. If possible, choose a thick gyoza skin.

Tofu Hot Pot with Star Anise

This simple Zen Buddhist vegan dish has the appetizing scent of star anise. The freeze-dried tofu (*koya dofu* in Japanese), soaked in soy milk, is delicious! You can also make it with atsu-age thick fried tofu or ganmodoki tofu fritters. You'll find the ingredients for this dish at your Japanese grocery. If you can't find mizuna greens, try arugula as a substitute.

SERVES 2

6–8 pieces freeze-dried tofu
Vegetable oil, for deep-frying
1¾ cups (400 ml) soy milk
1 star anise
⅔ teaspoon salt
½ bunch mizuna greens, about 3½ oz (100 g)

1 Put the freeze-dried tofu in a container in a single layer and add water to cover. Leave for 5–10 minutes and then change the water. Repeat this process 2–3 times until the tofu is soft, and then squeeze the pieces out well.
2 Heat the vegetable oil to 180°C (355°F), add the reconstituted freeze-dried tofu and deep-fry until golden brown. Drain off the oil.
3 Put the soy milk and star anise in a pot and bring to a boil over medium-low heat. Turn the heat down to low and partially cover the pot with a lid. Simmer for 5 minutes, taking care not to let the pot boil over. Season with the salt.
4 Add the Step 2 fried tofu to the Step 3 pot, top with the mizuna greens which have been cut into 2 inch (5cm) long pieces, and simmer briefly before serving.

After soaking the freeze-dried tofu, press it between the palms of your hands to squeeze out the water before frying.

Fry the tofu on both sides until it is a light golden brown.

Simmer the star anise for about 5 minutes to transfer its aroma to the soy milk.

Mochi, Miso and Soy Milk Hot Pot

The white miso gives a rich, hearty flavor to this meal. You can find lotus root, daikon radish sprouts, mochi rice cakes, dried gourd strips and readymade abura-age fried tofu pouches at your Asian or Japanese grocery—worth the trip for this delicious Japanese-style hot pot!

SERVES 2

3½ oz (100 g) lotus root

1 packet daikon radish sprouts, about ½ oz (15 g)

2 cups (500 ml) soy milk

3 tablespoons white miso

½ tablespoon toasted sesame oil

For the mochi pouches

2 square mochi rice cakes

4 kanpyo dried gourd strips, each 8 inches (20 cm) long

Salt, for sprinkling

2 abura-age fried tofu pouches

1 Make the mochi pouches. Cut the rice cakes in half. Briefly rinse the dried gourd strips, sprinkle with a little salt, and boil for 3–4 minutes. Cut the abura-age fried tofu pouches in half, open them into bags, and put half a piece of rice cake in each bag. Tie them up with the kanpyo strips.

2 Peel the lotus root and slice into ½ inch (1 cm) thick rounds. Trim and discard the roots from the daikon radish sprouts.

3 Put the soy milk in a pot over medium-low heat and bring to a boil. Add the lotus root slices, lower the heat, put the lid on the pot, and simmer for 5 minutes taking care that it doesn't boil over. Stir in the white miso and the toasted sesame oil. Serve topped with the daikon radish sprouts.

If you don't have kanpyo dried gourd strips, you can use toothpicks to hold the bags closed.

Once the mochi inside the tofu pouches has softened and the lotus root is cooked through, stir in the white miso.

Add toasted sesame oil to season. You can also add a sprinkle of coarsely ground black pepper if you like.

Pork Shabu-Shabu Soy Milk Hot Pot

This popular Japanese-style hot pot tastes great when made with soy milk, and the yuba tofu skin that forms on the surface is so good that you'll be fighting for your share! The homemade douchi sauce is a delicious accompaniment, but I also recommend simply sprinkling your serving with a little coarse salt.

SERVES 2

- 5½ oz (150 g) napa cabbage
- 9 oz (250 g) thinly sliced pork for shabu shabu
- 2 cups (500 ml) soy milk

For the douchi sauce

- 2 tablespoons douchi fermented soybeans (see page 56)
- 1 tablespoon untoasted sesame oil
- 2 tablespoons sake
- 2 tablespoons Chinese black vinegar (see below)

1 Cut the napa cabbage into large diagonal strips.

2 Make the douchi sauce. Put the douchi and sesame oil in a frying pan and stir-fry. When it is aromatic add the sake and black vinegar and mix. Turn off the heat and leave to cool.

3 Put the soy milk in a separate pot and bring to a boil over medium-low heat. Lower the heat, add the pork and napa cabbage and simmer briefly.

4 Serve in individual bowls topped with douchi sauce. An alternative to the sauce is to simply sprinkle the contents of your bowl with a little coarse salt.

Chinese black vinegar has a dark, smoky flavor. It is sometimes called Chinkiang vinegar or Zhenjiang vinegar. You can find it in Asian grocery stores and in some regular supermarkets.

Ramen with Chili Sauce

The delicious soup is both spicy and creamy. You can find fresh (or fresh-frozen) Chinese noodles at most Chinese or Asian grocery stores. The noodles are cooked briefly in boiling salted water before adding to the soup.

SERVES 2

2 eggs
7 oz (200 g) cabbage
1 tablespoon untoasted sesame oil
2 hanks fresh Chinese noodles

For the soup
2 cups (500 ml) soy milk
1 teaspoon chicken stock granules
¼ teaspoon salt
A little black pepper

For the chili oil
2 tablespoons chili pepper powder
1 tablespoon water
2 tablespoons toasted sesame oil

1 Make the chili oil. Put the chili pepper powder and water in a frying pan and mix. Add the toasted sesame oil turn the heat on low and heat until fragrant. Remove from the heat.
2 Hard-boil the eggs, peel and slice in half lengthwise. Shred the cabbage and stir-fry briefly in the untoasted sesame oil.
3 Make the soup. Put the soy milk and chicken stock granules in a pot and bring to a boil over medium-low heat. Turn the heat to low and simmer for about 5 minutes. Season with the salt and pepper.
4 Cook the noodles for 1–2 minutes in boiling salted water, drain and put into serving bowls. Ladle in the soup, top with the Step 2 ingredients, and drizzle with the Step 1 chili oil.

To make the chili oil, mix the chili pepper, water and sesame oil together over low heat until fragrant.

Briefly stir-fry the cabbage so that it's still crisp, but its sweetness has been brought out.

Adding chicken stock to soy milk makes a quick and easy soup for ramen.

Pork and Bean Sprout Ramen

The soup is made by boiling pork and using the broth as a base, giving it a rich, authentic flavor. Enjoy it with plenty of crunchy bean sprouts on top.

SERVES 2

2½ cups (250 g) bean sprouts
1 tablespoon untoasted sesame oil
Black pepper, to taste
2 hanks fresh Chinese noodles (see page 80)

For the boiled pork (an easy to make amount*)
14 oz (400 g) pork shoulder block
1¾ cups (400 ml) water
¾ cup (200 ml) sake
Black pepper, to taste
A few thin slices fresh ginger
Chopped green onion, to taste

For the soup
¾ cup (200 ml) of the pork cooking liquid
1¾ cups (400 ml) soy milk
2 tablespoons soy sauce

1 Make the boiled pork. Cut the pork shoulder block in half, boil it briefly then drain into a colander, reserving the drained liquid. Put the drained pork in a pot and add the water, sake, pepper, ginger and green onion. Bring the pot to a boil, turn the heat down and simmer for about 50 minutes. Turn off the heat and leave the pork to cool in the cooking liquid.
2 Make the soup. Put ¾ cup of the Step 1 pork cooking liquid and the 1¾ cups of soy milk into a pot and bring to a boil over medium-low heat. Reduce the heat and simmer for about 5 minutes. Season with the soy sauce.
3 Cut the thin stringy roots off the bean sprouts. Heat the untoasted sesame oil in a frying pan, briefly stir-fry the bean sprouts and sprinkle with black pepper.
4 Cook the noodles for 1–2 minutes in boiling salted water, drain and put into serving bowls. Ladle in the Step 2 soup and top with the bean sprouts. Slice the pork thinly and add 2 slices to each bowl.

*** Transfer the leftover boiled pork and cooking liquid to a storage container and refrigerate. It keeps for about two days.**

Boil the pork with sake, pepper, ginger and green onion. The key is to simmer over low heat.

Turn off the heat and let the pork cool in the cooking liquid. If you take it out of the liquid too soon, it will become tough.

The simple but tasty ramen soup is made with the pork cooking liquid, soy milk and soy sauce.

Miso Ramen with Chicken and Pickles

A hearty dish with tender, juicy steamed chicken. Soy milk is flavored with simple ingredients to create a tasty soup without the need for stock. It's garnished with zha cai pickles, made of preserved mustard stem, which you can find at your Chinese grocery.

SERVES 2

1 boneless chicken thigh, about 9 oz (250 g)

Black pepper, to taste

1 oz (30 g) zha cai pickles

2 hanks fresh Chinese noodles (see page 80)

For the soup

2 cups (500 ml) soy milk

2 tablespoons miso

A little black pepper

1 tablespoon toasted sesame oil

1 Sprinkle both sides of the chicken with the black pepper, place in a preheated steamer lined with kitchen parchment paper, and steam for about 20 minutes. Leave to cool down enough to handle, and cut into ½–1 inch (1–2 cm) strips.

2 Slice the zha cai pickle thinly.

3 Make the soup. Put the soy milk in a pot and bring to a boil over medium-low heat. Lower the heat and simmer for about 5 minutes. Stir in the miso until it dissolves. Season with the black pepper and the toasted sesame oil.

4 Cook the noodles for 1–2 minutes in boiling salted water, drain and put into serving bowls. Ladle in the soup and top with the chicken and pickles.

Sprinkle the chicken with pepper and steam it. It's a good idea to line the steamer with kitchen parchment paper first.

Steaming makes the chicken tender and easy to slice.

Dissolve the miso in the soy milk, and season with black pepper and toasted sesame oil. The soup is now complete.

Soy Milk Dan Dan Noodles

The combination of the soup, sautéed pork and spicy sauce is exquisite. It has a milky deliciousness even though it is spicy. I recommend making more of the sautéed pork and spicy sauce than you need for this recipe—leftovers can be refrigerated and used in other dishes.

SERVES 2

2 hanks fresh Chinese noodles (page 80)
1¾ cups (400 ml) soy milk
2 tablespoons ground white sesame seeds
Green onion, finely minced, for garnish

For the sautéed pork

1 tablespoon untoasted sesame oil
3½ oz (100 g) ground pork
1 tablespoon sake
1 tablespoon soy sauce

For the spicy sauce

2 tablespoons chili pepper powder
2 tablespoons toasted sesame oil
½ teaspoon Sichuan pepper powder
2 tablespoons soy sauce

1 Make the sautéed pork. Heat the untoasted sesame oil in a frying pan, put in the ground pork and sauté until cooked and crumbly. Season with the sake and soy sauce.
2 Make the spicy sauce. Put the chili pepper powder and toasted sesame oil in a pot over heat until fragrant. Add the Sichuan pepper powder and soy sauce and turn off the heat.
3 Cook the noodles for 1–2 minutes in boiling salted water, drain and put into serving bowls.
4 Put the soy milk in a pot and bring to a boil over medium-low heat. Remove from the heat, pour over the noodles, and top with the Step 1 sautéed pork and Step 2 spicy sauce. Sprinkle with the sesame seeds and green onion.

Sauté the pork thoroughly until it is crumbly, and season with sake and soy sauce.

The key to a successful spicy sauce is to cook it until fragrant.

Pour soy milk over the noodles, and top with the pork and the spicy sauce. Adjust the amount of spicy sauce to your liking.

Udon Noodles with Short Ribs and Coriander

A filling noodle dish that combines slow-cooked short ribs and fresh coriander. It has a flavor similar to tonkotsu pork-bone ramen broth, and goes well with thick noodles such as udon.

SERVES 2

7 oz (200 g) pork short ribs
¾ cup (200 ml) water
2 tablespoons sake
2 cups (500 ml) soy milk
½ teaspoon salt
2 packets frozen udon noodles
Fresh coriander, roughly chopped, for garnish

1 Boil the short ribs briefly, then drain them. Put them in a pot, add the water and sake, and bring to a boil. Turn the heat to low, cover the pot with a lid and simmer for about 30 minutes.
2 Add the soy milk to the pot and simmer for another 5 minutes, then season with the salt.
3 Bring a pan of water to a boil, put in the udon noodles for 1–2 minutes, then drain.
4 Arrange the udon noodles in bowls, top with the short ribs, and pour in the soup. Garnish with the roughly chopped coriander.

Simmering the short ribs gently over low heat ensures that they are tender.

While simmering the soy milk, remove any scum rises to the surface.

After simmering for 5 minutes the soup is done. Pour it piping hot over the udon noodles.

Soy Milk and Crab Udon Noodles

It's a little extravagant, but this is one of my favorite noodle dishes. The key to its delicious flavor is sautéing the green onion first, then adding the crab and sautéing it as well to bring out its rich umami before simmering.

SERVES 2

- 2 packets frozen udon noodles
- 1 packet boiled crab legs in their shells, about 2 lb 2 oz (1 kg)
- 1 large green onion
- 1 tablespoon untoasted sesame oil
- 2 cups (500 ml) soy milk
- ½ teaspoon salt
- Black pepper, to taste

1 Bring a pan of water to a boil, put in the udon noodles for 1–2 minutes, then drain.

2 If the crab legs are large, cut into bite-size pieces. Slice the green onion thinly.

3 Put the untoasted sesame oil and green onion in a pot and stir-fry. When the onion is fragrant, add the crab legs and stir-fry briefly.

4 Add the soy milk to the pot. When it comes to a boil turn the heat to low and simmer for about 5 minutes.

5 Add the cooked udon noodles from Step 1 and simmer for another 2 minutes. Season with the salt and pepper.

Nyumen Noodles with Soy Milk and Tofu

Somen are thin, wheat-flour Japanese noodles, served chilled in summer. The hot version is called nyumen, and this dish, flavored with ginger and leeks, is a real treat for body and soul.

SERVES 2

2–3 bundles dried somen noodles
1 piece ginger
4 inch (10 cm) length green onion
1 small dried red chili pepper
1 tablespoon untoasted sesame oil
1¾ cups (400 ml) soy milk
1 block silken tofu, about 12 oz (350 g)
½ teaspoon salt

1 Bring a large pot of water to a boil, and put in the noodles for 2–3 minutes. Drain into a colander and rinse under running water. Drain well.

2 Finely mince the ginger and green onion. Crush the red chili pepper.

3 Heat the untoasted sesame oil and the Step 2 ingredients in a pot. When it is fragrant add the soy milk. Then add the tofu while crumbling it in by hand. Bring the pot to a boil, then lower the heat to a simmer for about 5 minutes. Season with the salt.

4 Add the noodles to the pot, and simmer for about 1 minute before serving.

Shrimp Macaroni au Gratin

Béchamel sauce made with soy milk is surprisingly rich, flavorful and creamy. Even people who don't like soy milk will be fine with this. You can also pour it over rice and make it into a rice gratin. If you want to keep this dish non-dairy, use vegan cheese.

SERVES 2

3½ oz (100 g) dried macaroni
3½ oz (100 g) peeled shrimp
2 tablespoons butter
2 tablespoons flour
1¾ cups (400 ml) soy milk
⅓ teaspoon salt
2 oz (50 g) grated vegan cheese

1 Boil the macaroni in salted hot water for the time stated on the packet and drain. Boil the shrimp briefly.
2 Put the butter and flour in a frying pan over heat, and sauté until fragrant. Add the soy milk a little at a time to make a smooth sauce. Season with the salt.
3 Take the frying pan off the heat and add the macaroni and shrimp from Step 1. Mix well and transfer to an ovenproof baking dish.
4 Top with the cheese, and bake for 8 minutes at 110°F (230°C) until browned on top.

Once the butter and flour have been mixed together, gradually add the soy milk to make a smooth béchamel sauce.

Add the macaroni and shrimp and mix with the béchamel sauce.

Top with the cheese. You can sprinkle on some breadcrumbs too.

Rice Porridge with Goji Berries

Goji berries are an essential ingredient in Chinese herbal medicine, and have long been considered a wonder drug for longevity and a great pick-me-up. They have a subtle sweetness, slight acidity and a fruity flavor.

SERVES 2

- 6½ tablespoons uncooked short-grain Japanese rice (often labeled "sushi rice")
- 1¼ cups (300 ml) water
- 1¾ cups (400 ml) soy milk
- 1 tablespoon goji berries

1 Rinse the rice and drain into a colander.

2 Put the rice and the 1¼ cups of water into a pot and bring to a boil. Turn the heat to low, partially cover the pot with a lid, and simmer for 20 minutes, taking care not to let it boil over.

3 Add the soy milk and mix, then simmer for another 20 minutes. Put in the goji berries and simmer for another 5 minutes before serving.

After simmering the rice for about 20 minutes, add the soy milk and simmer for another 20 minutes to finish the rice porridge

Rice Porridge with Scallops

This popular porridge is infused with the rich, concentrated flavor of scallops, whose savory aroma is delightfully enticing. The porridge is seasoned simply with just salt and sesame oil. You can find dried scallops at your Asian grocery store.

SERVES 2

- 6½ tablespoons uncooked short-grain Japanese rice (often labeled "sushi rice")
- 6 small dried scallops
- 1¼ cups (300 ml) water
- 1¾ cups (400 ml) soy milk
- ⅓ teaspoon salt
- ½ tablespoon toasted sesame oil

1 Rinse the rice and drain into a colander. Reconstitute the scallops in water overnight, drain and shred.

2 Put the Step 1 ingredients and the 1¼ cups of water into a pot and bring to a boil. Turn the heat to low, partially cover the pot with a lid, and simmer for 20 minutes, taking care not to let it boil over.

3 Add the soy milk and mix, then simmer for another 20 minutes. Season with the salt and the toasted sesame oil.

Soak the scallops in water overnight to reconstitute. They taste better when reconstituted slowly.

Rice Porridge with Century Egg

This unique porridge is made with a rich-tasting century egg—an egg that has been preserved in clay, ash and salt for weeks or months, turning the white gelatinous and dark, and the yolk green. You can buy century eggs in the refrigerated section of your Chinese grocery store.

SERVES 2

- 6½ tablespoons uncooked short-grain Japanese rice (often labeled "sushi rice")
- 1¼ cups (300 ml) water
- 1¾ cups (400 ml) soy milk
- 1 century egg
- 1 tablespoon soy sauce
- 1 tablespoon toasted sesame oil
- 2 lettuce leaves

1 Rinse the rice and drain into a colander.

2 Put the rice and the 1¼ cups of water into a pot and bring to a boil. Turn the heat to low, partially cover the pot with a lid, and simmer for 20 minutes, taking care not to let it boil over. Add the soy milk and simmer for another 20 minutes.

3 Chop the century egg into bite-size pieces, and mix with the soy sauce and toasted sesame oil. Chop up the lettuce roughly.

4 Add the lettuce to the Step 2 pot and simmer briefly. Add the century egg mixture and mix.

The century egg gives the porridge a rich, mellow flavor.

Rice Porridge with Fermented Tofu

Enriched with the deep, cheese-like richness of fermented tofu, this porridge has a distinctive taste, with the unique deliciousness that only fermented foods can provide. It is a standard food in China. You can get fermented tofu from your Asian grocery store.

SERVES 2

- 6½ tablespoons uncooked short-grain Japanese rice (often labeled "sushi rice")
- 1¼ cups (300 ml) water
- 1¾ cups (400 ml) soy milk
- 1 oz (30 g) fermented tofu
- 1 tablespoon toasted sesame oil

1 Rinse the rice and drain into a colander.

2 Put the rice and the 1¼ cups of water into a pot and bring to a boil. Turn the heat to low, partially cover the pot with a lid, and simmer for 20 minutes, taking care not to let it boil over.

3 Add the soy milk and mix in, and simmer for another 20 minutes. Crumble in the fermented tofu, and season with the toasted sesame oil.

The fermented tofu is added when the porridge is cooked. You can adjust the amount according to your taste.

Rice Porridge with Oolong Tea

Oolong tea leaves are rich in vitamins, and make a nutritious and fragrant addition to rice porridge. For this porridge, use short-grain glutinous rice, sometimes labeled "sweet rice," "sticky rice," or "mochi rice."

SERVES 2

6½ tablespoons uncooked glutinous rice

1 teaspoon oolong tea leaves

1¼ cups (300 ml) water

1¾ cups (400 ml) soy milk

1 Rinse the rice and drain into a colander.

2 Pound the oolong tea leaves and put into a bowl. Add enough hot water to cover and let the leaves soften. Drain.

3 Put the 1¼ cups of water and Step 1 rice into a pot and bring to a boil. Turn the heat down to low, partially cover the pot with a lid, and simmer for 20 minutes, taking care not to let it boil over.

4 Add the soy milk and simmer for another 20 minutes. Add the Step 2 tea leaves and simmer for another 10 minutes before serving.

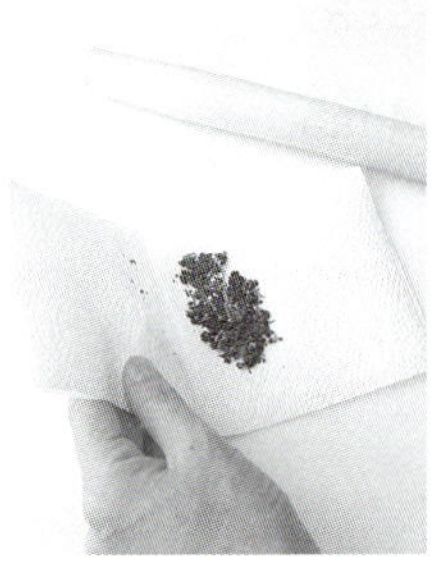

If you pound the tea leaves, they will release more flavor and nutrients.

Brown Rice Porridge with Tangerine Peel

This porridge, made with *chenpi*—dried tangerine peel commonly used to prevent colds—is perfect for winter. The chenpi also adds a refreshing citrus aroma. You can find chenpi at your Asian grocery store. Brown rice is used to make this porridge.

SERVES 2

- 4 tablespoons uncooked short-grain brown rice
- 1–2 pieces dried tangerine peel
- 2½ cups (600 ml) water
- 1¾ cups (400 ml) soy milk

1 Rinse the brown rice, leave to soak in plenty of water overnight, then drain. Chop the chenpi into small pieces.
2 Put the Step 1 brown rice and chenpi and the 2½ cups of water into a pot and bring to a boil. Turn the heat to low and partially cover the pot with a lid. Simmer for 40–50 minutes, taking care that it doesn't boil over.
3 Add the soy milk and mix. Simmer for another 20 minutes before serving.

Brown rice should be soaked in water overnight before making into porridge.

Black Rice Soy Milk Porridge

Black rice—also known as "forbidden rice"—is said to have been a favorite beauty food of Yang Guifei, consort of Emperor Xuanzong during the Tang dynasty. She is known as one of the Four Beauties of ancient China. This simple porridge is nutritious, naturally sweet and has a great fragrance. Try it served with a little jelly or brown sugar.

SERVES 2

½ cup (100 g) medium-grain black rice

2½ cups (600 ml) water

1¾ cups (400 ml) soy milk

1 Rinse the rice and soak in plenty of water overnight.

2 Drain the rice well. Put the rice and the 2½ cups of water in a pot and bring to a boil. Turn the heat to low, partially cover the pot with a lid, and simmer for 20 minutes, taking care not to let it boil over.

3 Add the soy milk, and simmer for another 20 minutes before serving.

First, cook the black rice in water. Then add soy milk and continue simmering.

Oatmeal Soy Milk Porridge

Oatmeal is great for porridge because it's rich in iron, calcium and dietary fiber. This version is very simple, but you could also sprinkle in some dried fruit or nuts.

SERVES 2

¾ cup (60 g) oatmeal
¾ cup (200 ml) water
1¾ cups (400 ml) soy milk
Salt, to taste

1 Put the oatmeal and the ¾ cup of water into a pot and leave for 5 minutes to let the oatmeal absorb the water.
2 Add soy milk to the pot, turn on the heat to medium-low, and stir to mix. When the pot comes to a boil reduce the heat and partially cover the pot with a lid. Simmer for 5 minutes, taking care not to let it boil over.
3 When you have a creamy porridge, turn off the heat, and season with salt.

Let the oatmeal absorb the soaking water before adding the soy milk.

Mushrooms Stewed in Honey Soy Milk

In China, white wood ear mushrooms are often stewed in a sweet sauce and served as a dessert. This is a dish that adds a little twist to this classic, using soy milk and honey for a creamy texture. Find dried wood ear mushrooms in your Asian grocery.

AN EASY TO MAKE AMOUNT

½ oz (15 g) dried white wood ear mushrooms
1¾ cups (400 ml) water
3 tablespoons honey
¾ cup (200 ml) soy milk
Cinnamon powder, to taste

1 Soak the mushrooms in water for about 30 minutes to rehydrate. Drain well, and remove the tough stems.
2 Put the mushrooms and the 1¾ cups of water in a pot. Bring to a boil, lower the heat, put on a lid, and simmer for about 30 minutes. Turn off the heat.
3 Let the mushrooms soak in the pot for 1 hour. Add the honey, and bring the pot back to a boil. Lower the heat and simmer for 10 minutes. Mix in the soy milk. Serve sprinkled with cinnamon powder.

Reconstitute the wood ear mushrooms in water for at least 30 minutes.

Mung Beans with Soy Milk

Mung beans are common in Chinese and Southeast Asian dishes. They have a natural sweetness so they work well for desserts. Here, they're combined with soy milk and coconut to create an Asian-style sweet soup. You can use adzuki beans instead of mung beans.

AN EASY TO MAKE AMOUNT

¾ cup (150 g) mung beans
2½ cups (600 ml) water
5 tablespoons raw cane sugar
1¾ cups (400 ml) soy milk
1 tablespoon shredded coconut

1 Rinse the mung beans and put into a pot with the 2½ cups of water. Bring to a boil, turn the heat down to low, cover the pot with a lid and simmer for about 20 minutes.
2 Turn off the heat, and leave to soak for about an hour.
3 Put the pot back on the heat, add the sugar and simmer over low heat for about 30 minutes. Add the soy milk and simmer for an additional 10 minutes.
4 Ladle into serving bowls and garnish with the shredded coconut.

The combination of naturally sweet mung beans, sugar and soy milk makes for a delicious dessert.

Soy Milk Almond Jelly

This almond jelly is sure to become a fast favorite. Simply mix the ingredients over heat, pour into serving dishes and chill in the refrigerator to set—easy and fuss-free!

SERVES 2–3

⅓ cup (40 g) almond flour

6½ tablespoons water

1 scant tablespoon agar powder

1¼ cups (300 ml) soy milk

2 heaping tablespoons raw cane sugar

Goji berries, for garnish

1 Put almond flour in a pot and add the 6½ tablespoons of water a little at a time while stirring to dissolve. Add the agar powder and mix well.

2 Add the soy milk and sugar to the pot. Turn on the heat to medium-low, and cook while stirring. Turn off the heat just before the pot comes to a boil.

3 Pour into serving dishes. When it has cooled down a bit refrigerate to set. Garnish with goji berries to serve.

For best results, use a whisk to stir the ingredients while they are being heated in Step 2.

Dried Figs with Soy Milk

A simple recipe for steamed dried fruit soaked in soy milk. You can also use dried figs, dried apricots or dried mangoes. Feel free to add a touch of cinnamon or star anise for extra flavor.

AN EASY TO MAKE AMOUNT

5 oz (150 g) dried figs
1¼ cups (300 ml) soy milk

1 Place the dried figs in a preheated steamer lined with kitchen parchment paper. Steam for 20 minutes.
2 Put the soy milk in a pot over medium-low heat. Once it comes to a boil, add the steamed figs and turn off the heat.
3 Let the pot cool down, then transfer the contents to an airtight container and refrigerate for a day before serving.

This is the perfect snack to have stored in the refrigerator if ever you're craving something sweet.

My Family's Soy Milk Pudding

I like to make soy milk pudding flavored with fennel, an herb often used in Chinese medicine that is said to aid digestion and be good for weight loss. It gives a distinctive flavor and a refreshing aroma to this comforting and healthy dessert—one of my family's favorites.

SERVES 2–3

2 eggs

1¾ cups (400 ml) soy milk

5 tablespoons raw cane sugar

Pinch fennel powder

Molasses, to serve

Kinako roasted soybean flour (see page 16), to serve

1 Break the eggs into a bowl, and add the soy milk, raw cane sugar and fennel powder in that order and mix.

2 Strain the mixture through a fine-mesh sieve to smooth it out, and pour into heatproof serving dishes.

3 Place the serving dishes in a preheated steamer. Steam over high heat for about 5 minutes, then over low heat for 10 minutes.

4 Serve topped with molasses and sprinkled with kinako.

The key to a smooth and creamy dessert is to strain the mixture carefully in Step 2.

Soft Soy Milk Cookies

These are cookies, but they are soft and moist! The tender texture makes them an irresistible treat. Soy milk is added to make a very soft dough, which is then spooned out onto a baking sheet and baked in the oven.

MAKES 8 COOKIES

1 egg

1⅔ oz (50 g) room-temperature butter

4 tablespoons raw cane sugar

1 tablespoon baking powder

1 tablespoon almond flour

1 pinch baking soda

¾ cup (100 g) cake flour

3½ tablespoons soy milk

8 roasted whole almonds

1 Beat the egg.

2 Cream the butter and sugar together in a bowl. Add half the beaten egg and mix.

3 Add the baking powder, almond flour and baking soda to the Step 2 mixture and mix well. Add the cake flour and the soy milk in that order and mix.

4 Line a baking sheet with kitchen parchment paper, divide the Step 3 mixture into 8 portions and drop on the kitchen parchment paper with a spoon.

5 Brush the remaining beaten egg on top of the 8 portions of dough, top each one in the middle with an almond, and bake at 355°F (180°C) for about 12 minutes.

The cookie dough is so soft and moist that you need to scoop it with a spoon to place on the baking sheet.

Chinese-style Soy Milk Doughnuts

Chinese doughnuts are known for their firm, satisfying texture and the fact that, despite being fried, they're not greasy—that's part of their appeal. The secret to their deliciousness lies in deep-frying them slowly in low-temperature oil.

8 DOUGHNUTS

- 1 egg
- 1¾ cups (200 g) cake flour
- ½ tablespoon baking powder
- 4 tablespoons raw cane sugar
- 3½ tablespoons soy milk
- Untoasted white sesame seeds, for coating
- Untoasted sesame oil, or other vegetable oil, for deep-frying

1 Break the egg into a bowl. Add the flour, baking powder and sugar, and mix. Add the soy milk and mix well to form a dough.

2 Divide the dough into 8 portions and form each into a ball. Coat each with sesame seeds.

3 Heat the frying oil to 300–329°F (150–160°C), Put the dough balls gently in the oil, and deep-fry them slowly while gradually raising the temperature.

4 When the doughnuts are golden brown, take them out, drain off the oil, and place on a rack to drain off any excess oil before serving.

The sesame seeds add a great nutty flavor.

Soy Milk Ma Lai Gao Sponge Cake

Ma Lai Gao is a Chinese sponge cake. It is very easy to make, as you just mix the ingredients and steam them. You can eat it hot straight from the oven, or you can let it cool and eat it sliced. It's a flavor you'll never get tired of!

AN EASY TO MAKE AMOUNT

- 3 eggs
- 5 tablespoons raw cane sugar
- 3½ tablespoons soy milk
- ¾ cup (100 g) cake flour
- 1 tablespoon baking powder
- 2 tablespoons untoasted sesame oil

1 Beat the eggs in a bowl. Add the sugar and soy milk and mix.
2 Add the cake flour and baking powder to the bowl and mix. Mix in the untoasted sesame oil. This is the cake batter.
3 Line a preheated bamboo steamer with kitchen parchment paper, and pour in the batter.
4 Steam for 18–20 minutes making sure it is cooked through to the center. Remove from the steamer and serve hot or cool.

For this quantity of ingredients I use a bamboo steamer about 7 inches (18 cm) in diameter.

Index of Main Ingredients

"Books to Span the East and West"

Tuttle Publishing was founded in 1832 in the small New England town of Rutland, Vermont [USA]. Our core values remain as strong today as they were then—to publish best-in-class books which bring people together one page at a time. In 1948, we established a publishing outpost in Japan—and Tuttle is now a leader in publishing English-language books about the arts, languages and cultures of Asia. The world has become a much smaller place today and Asia's economic and cultural influence has grown. Yet the need for meaningful dialogue and information about this diverse region has never been greater. Over the past seven decades, Tuttle has published thousands of books on subjects ranging from martial arts and paper crafts to language learning and literature—and our talented authors, illustrators, designers and photographers have won many prestigious awards. We welcome you to explore the wealth of information available on Asia at **www.tuttlepublishing.com**.

Published by Tuttle Publishing, an imprint of Periplus Editions (HK) Ltd.

www.tuttlepublishing.com

Tonyu Karada wo Totonoeru Kihon no Shokuzai

ISBN: 978-0-8048-5908-0

28 27 26 25
10 9 8 7 6 5 4 3 2 1

Printed in China 2507EP

Distributed by
North America, Latin America & Europe
Tuttle Publishing
364 Innovation Drive
North Clarendon, VT 05759-9436 U.S.A.
Tel: 1 (802) 773 8930 | Fax: 1 (802) 773 6993
info@tuttlepublishing.com
www.tuttlepublishing.com

Japan
Tuttle Publishing
Yaekari Building 3rd Floor
5-4-12 Osaki
Shinagawa-ku
Tokyo 141-0032
Tel: (81) 3 5437 0171 | Fax: (81) 3 5437 0755
sales@tuttle.co.jp
www.tuttle.co.jp

Asia Pacific
Berkeley Books Pte. Ltd.
3 Kallang Sector #04-01
Singapore 349278
Tel: (65) 6741 2178 | Fax: (65) 6741 2179
inquiries@periplus.com.sg
www.tuttlepublishing.com

GPSR representative
Matt Parsons
matt.parsons@upi2mbooks.hr
UPI-2M PLUS d.o.o., Medulićeva 20, 10000 Zagreb, Croatia